WHERE ARE WE GOING?

Written & Un-Edited
by Darick Spears

Where are we going?
Based on the News Anchor,
We are going to war.
The world is in a state of
emergency,
And no one seems to give a
damn.
All eyes are glued to the cell
phone screen,
It is so easy to communicate,
But no one is saying a thing.

Broken glass everywhere,
As feet trample across bloody rivers,
And we can't seem to get over the word "nigger."
To be honest I see none.
When I stare into the eyes of the next human being,
I see myself.
So, I treat them as such.

Where are we going?
The world is plagued with racism.
You can't cover hatred up with good deeds.
Purge your heart,
Open your mind,
Ask the questions that you desire to be answered.

Let's go out to dinner,
I'll pay for your meal.
Explain to me your culture,
Your likes and dislikes,
Your philosophies- your religion,
And don't be offended if mines differ.

Where are we going?
Are the schools finally going to open up?
Are people going to actually go back to work?
Is unemployment finally gonna give us our back pay?
Is the government going to use vaseline next time?

Are you honest?
Do you really tell yourself the truth?
If you can't be true to yourself,
Then you can't be true to others.
So, I ask you again -
Are you honest?
We can't go anywhere if you are not
willing to be real.

Where are we going?
Is it safe to park my car in front of my house at night?
Is it safe to dial 9-1-1?
Is it safe to accept a friend request on Facebook?
Hold on,
Someone is ringing my doorbell.

Where are we going?
Have you put your trust in the right entity?
Is the ground that you are standing on sinking sand?
I have learned to hold on to God's unchanging hand.
He is the wisest compass.

The easiest thing to do is listen.
The hardest thing to do is to hear.
Feel compassion,
Empathy,
And then to let your feet take mobility.
That's putting words to action,
That's changing the world one step at
a time.

Where are we going?
I hope the answer is "to Heaven."
Then the question becomes,
How do we get there?
Have you followed the roadmap?
Have you heard that there is a
book full of the Good News?
What is the Good News you may
ask?
It is the Gospel.

Did you know that the Good Book
has been scattered?
There are missing pieces to the
puzzle.
But I warn you not to panic
because of man's schemes,
Because the lost pieces are
available.
Search and you will find answers.

Where are we going?
I hear that there is a huge
wedding coming soon,
The groom is searching for
his bride.
One who wears linen without a
spot or wrinkle,
One who is found honorable.
Do you have your outfit
ready?

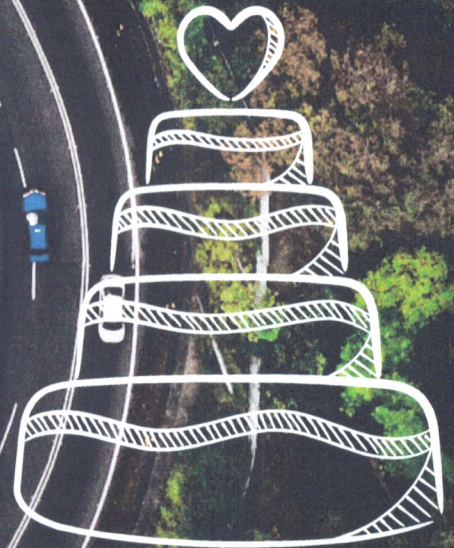

Some sell their souls for material gain,
I have offered my soul for eternal entrance.
I had to submit,
I had to confess out of my mouth,
I had to believe in my heart.
Then my soul was saved.

Where are we going?
We have to travel to and fro,
We need to stroll through the highways and dark avenues.
Let your hand embrace another hand,
Let your arms secure another.
Love in action.

The sudden rush of thought can spark the greatest action.
Are you using your mind?
Are you obeying your inner ambition?
Because where we are going diversity is respected.
And where we are going your opinion matters.

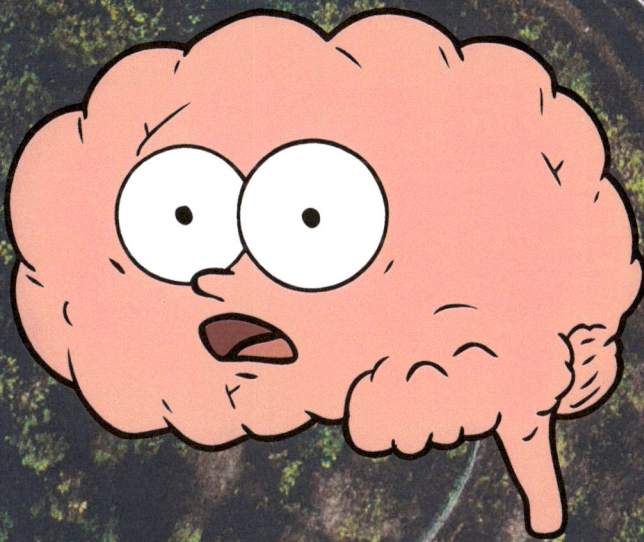

Where are we going?
Is there a new mindstate?
Is there a new diet involved?
Is there a plan to forgive?
Is there a new opportunity
to commit to?
It's never too late to start
over,
Until it's over.

Let's go out and witness,
Let's tell of the goodness of
the Lord.
Let's go to a new business
and support.
Let's do something positive
today.
Aren't you tired of division?
Hatred comes in multiples.

Attitude creates
temperature,
Patience births peace and
experience.
Love conquers all.
Where are we going?
I hope not to another
protest.

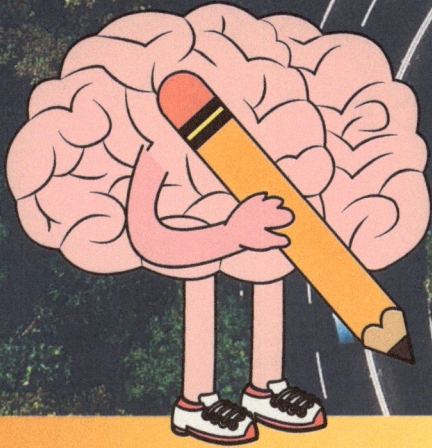

I hope we are not going to another funeral,
Especially over senseless violence.
Let's all go out and vote,
It does make a difference.
Let us think different,
As well as become the difference.

Let's move forward,
Never backward.
Let's let the past be the past,
Let's focus on the present.
Let's push the envelope and change some things for the best.
Let's be the change we wish to see.

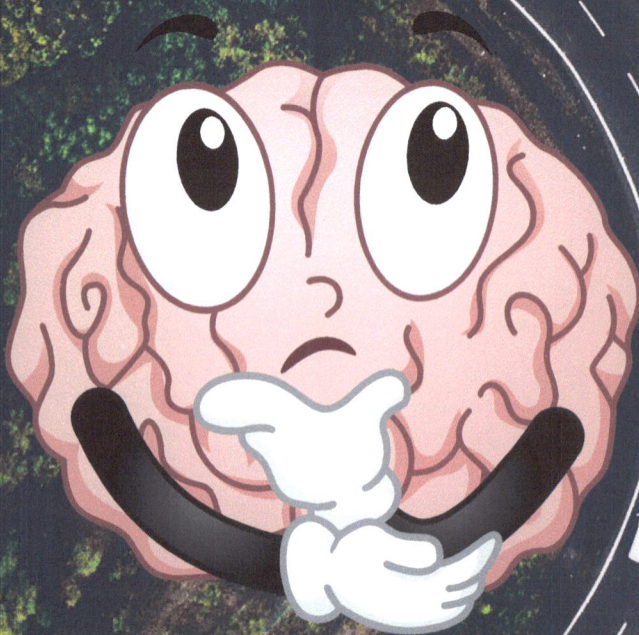

Where Are We Going?

BY DARICK SPEARS

Darick Books

THE FIRST BOOKSTORE OF ITS KIND

BY DARICK SPEARS